PENGUIN BOOKS
THE BEST OF LAXMAN

R.K. Laxman was born and educated in Mysore. Soon after he graduated from the University of Mysore, he started drawing cartoons for the *Free Press Journal,* a newspaper in Bombay. Six months later he joined the *Times of India,* a newspaper he has been with, as staff cartoonist, for the past 40 years. He has written and published several short stories, essays and travel articles. Some of these were published in a book, *Idle Hours.* He has also published eight collections of his cartoons.

Mr Laxman was awarded the prestigious Padma Bhushan by the Government of India. The University of Marathwada conferred an honorary Doctor of Literature degree on him. He has won several awards for his cartoons, including Asia's top journalism award, the Ramon Magsaysay award, in 1984.

R.K. Laxman lives in Bombay.

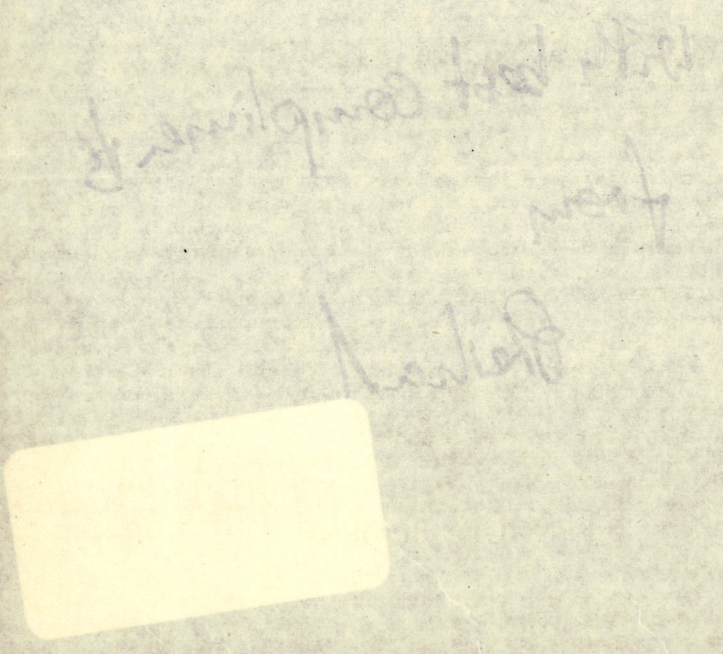

R. K. LAXMAN

The Best of Laxman

PENGUIN BOOKS

Penguin Books India(P)Limited,72-B Himalaya House, 23 Kasturba Gandhi Marg,
New Delhi 110 001, India
Penguin Books Ltd., Harmondsworth, Middlesex, England
Viking Penguin USA Inc., 375 Hudson Street, New York 10014, U.S.A.
Penguin Books Australia Ltd., Ringwood, Victoria, Australia
Penguin Books Canada Ltd., 2801 John Street, Markham, Ontario, Canada L3R 1 B4
Penguin Books (N.Z.) Ltd., 182–190 Wairau Road, Auckland 10, New Zealand

First published by Penguin Books India 1990

Reprinted 1991, 1992

Copyright © R.K. Laxman 1990

All rights reserved

Made and printed in India by Ananda Offset Private Ltd., Calcutta

Some of these cartoons appeared in *You Said It* volumes 1,2,3,4,5,6 and 7 published by India Book House. Grateful acknowledgements are made to the publishers for the permission to reproduce these cartoons. All the cartoons in this book first appeared in the *Times of India*.

This book is sold subject to the condition that it shall not, by way of trade or otherwise, be lent, resold, hired out, or otherwise circulated without the publisher's prior written consent in any form of binding or cover other than that in which it is published and without a similar condition including this condition being imposed on the subsequent purchaser and without limiting the rights under copyright reserved above, no part of this publication may be reproduced, stored in or introduced into a retrieval system, or transmitted in any form or by any means (electronic, mechanical, photocopying, recording or otherwise), without the prior written permission of both the copyright owner and the above mentioned publisher of this book.

Introduction

Just over a century ago the art of cartooning came here from England and struck roots. Although other forms of art like sculpture, carving, poetry, painting and drawing had been flourishing in India for centuries, the art of graphic satire and humour was unknown. Of course satire and humour did exist in folklore and poetry, poking fun at the follies of men and monarchs, but the funny antics and humorous articles of the classical court-jester were really satirical comments used to gently bring a wayward king and his band of courtiers back on the track.

The role of today's cartoonist is not unlike that of the court-jester of yore. His business in a democracy is to exercise his right to criticize, ridicule, demolish, complain and find fault with the administration and political leaders, through caricatures and cartoons.

When the British ruled, the freedom allowed to the press was limited. Editorial comments and cartoons were largely confined to tackling social evils like child marriage, child labour and the dowry system, or in praising the efforts of the reformers. They hardly ever touched on political subjects.

Some years later the Indian cartoonist began to make timid inroads into political matters. But he only attacked symbols, John Bull, for instance. (Enslaved India was symbolized by an image of a suffering Indian woman called Bharatmata.)

When the Indian National Movement began to gather momentum the cartoonist gained the courage to depict real characters: the political leaders, the viceroys and governors who were the guardians of the imperial authority.

When the British left, our leaders, who had fought for freedom, settled down to draw up a respectable Constitution to ensure freedom and equal status to people who had been denied democratic liberty for centuries. India was declared a sovereign secular republic in which every citizen was supposed to enjoy equality, fraternity and liberty. The freedom of the press became particularly sacred. It was one of the most important checks on our democratic institutions. Having drawn up such a magnificent Constitution the leaders and the led sat themselves down and looked forward to a life of peace and prosperity.

If things had worked the way our founding fathers had hoped, the cartoonist would long ago have become an extinct species. Fortunately for the cartoonist, both the rulers and the ruled unintentionally became champions of the cartoonist's cause and ceaselessly provided grist to his mill.

When Nehru took over as Prime Minister it soon became apparent to the cartoonist that he could look forward to an exciting career ahead. The aspirations of linguistic chauvinists, cow-protectors, prohibitionists, name-changers of parks and streets, all began to make their ludicrous appearance on the national scene. The number of satirical cartoonists increased rapidly. Our political activities became equally uproarious from the satirical point of view. Our leaders injected an altogether new style of functioning in our political life—hitherto unknown to the ordinary citizen. News about political parties did not concern their ideologies or their plans to help the common man, but detailed instead how intra-party groups worked against each other, or squabbled amongst themselves, or parted company from the party and formed a new party, or defected to the very party they had opposed tooth and nail until that moment. All this led to curiouser and curiouser political behaviour—*dharnas*, floor-crossing, booth-capturing, 'toppling' a Chief Minister, and what-have-you. Naturally, a cartoonist, even one with limited talent, could flourish effortlessly. So within a decade of independence the tribe of cartoonists proliferated. New dailies, weeklies and fortnightlies, in every feasible language mushroomed everywhere, thus opening up vast opportunities for the cartoonist.

As a nation we are rather prone to talk politics; whether at a bus-stand or in a railway compartment, hobnobbing at an exclusive cocktail party or jogging in a public park. Of course, what passes for politics in these sessions is really gossip—rumour, hearsay or scandal rooted in some blurred misinterpretation of facts—concocted into a palatable mixture that is masticated between reading newspapers and political magazines and listening to political comments on the radio. That is why, though not all Indian publications are political in content, most of these allow for a page or two of political satire and caricature, in acknowledgement of this national pastime. Thus, the country which didn't have a single cartoonist less than a century ago is now swarming with them: good, bad and indifferent.

As I became more and more entrenched in watching and commenting on the political phantasmagoria of our country I needed an acceptable symbol to define the common Indian in my cartoons.

For the cartoonist time is of the essence and the political cartoonist has the Damocles' Sword of deadlines permanently hanging over his head. Many precious minutes would be lost if he were to draw elaborate masses of people composed of Maharashtrians, Bengalis, Tamilians, Punjabis and Assamese. It is easy for the cartoonist in the West where the dress and appearance of people are largely standardized, but in India there is no way of classifying an individual by the dress he wears. An industrialist, say a textile tycoon, may be dressed exactly like a retail fruit seller. Or again, a scholar of Sanskrit, English, Greek and Latin might look like the humble priest of an old impoverished temple. So how was I to discover and portray the common denomination in this medley of characters, dresses, appearances and habits?

In the early days I used to hurriedly cram in as many figures as I could to represent the masses. Gradually my efforts narrowed to fewer and fewer figures. These my readers came to accept as representative of the whole country. Finally, I succeeded in reducing my symbol to one man: a man in a checked coat, whose bald head boasts only a wisp of white hair, and whose bristling moustache lends support to a bulbous nose, which in turn holds up an oversized pair of glasses. He has a permanent look of bewilderment on his face. He is ubiquitous. Today he is found hanging around a cabinet-room where a high-powered meeting is in progress. Tomorrow he is among the slum-dwellers listening to their woes or is marching along with protestors as they demand the abolition of the nuclear bomb. That, of course, would not preclude him from being present at a banquet hosted by the Prime Minister for a visiting foreign dignitary! This man has survived all sorts of domestic crises for forty years, while the politicians who professed to protect him have long disappeared. He is tough and durable. Like the mute millions of our country he has not uttered a word in all the years he's been around. He is a silent, bewildered, and often bemused, spectator of events which anyway are beyond his control.

Besides my usual 'big' cartoons I started a series called *You Said It*. A single column cartoon appeared every day in the *Times of India* in its slotted place, the right hand corner of the front page. The idea was to make it a free-wheeling comment on socio-economic and socio-political aspects, free of real political personalities or factual political events. The feature did not attempt any serious analysis but reflected, with a certain conscious irreverence, the general mood of the country as a whole. I expected this column to appeal to readers who were not too critical and who accepted their humdrum lot without a murmur. My taciturn Common Man, who was appearing off and on in my bigger cartoons in the company of Jawaharlal Nehru and his cabinet ministers, came in handy for this purpose. The other characters I built around him in this single column cartoon were villagers, bureaucrats, ministers, crooked businessmen, economic experts, rebellious students, factory workers—in fact nearly every type, from every walk of life, as the occasion warranted it. *You Said It* proved extremely popular. It has appeared every day for more than three decades except on those all-too-brief occasions when I am on holiday!

Cartooning is the art of disapproval and complaint. It treats men and matters with a certain healthy scepticism and good-humoured ridicule, but never malice. A cartoon attempts to preserve the sense of humour of the community which is so essential for survival in day-to-day existence.

Gathered in this volume is a selection from thousands of cartoons I have done over the years. I am continually surprised to note that most of them are timeless in their relevance to any given moment in our history.

5 August, 1990　　　　　　　　　　　　　　　　　　　　*R.K. Laxman*

Don't threaten me! You are incapable of hitting anything with that bat.

Why am I going abroad? To study the conditions in our country of course!

There must be some sort of civic life up there — look at all those pits and pot-holes...

Say, I did not have time to check — what progress have we made since 1947?

I just asked the candidate to draw a chair and sit down!

You are Gangaram Vinayak? There's a letter for you — Shri Gangaram Vinayak, care of Sir William Jack, CIE, OBE, Bombay.

Oh, you are all utterly ungrateful — clear out of the house at once!

Please turn this way and make your address, Sir. Those are the organizers.

In spite of all our efforts there's still a large stock of unsold cloth with us!

Of course, I have a car. But, I don't have a road to drive it on!

The Minister is going via Rome, Paris, London, New York and Tokyo to Calcutta to attend a conference there.

...eradication of desires, self-abnegation and relentless pursuit of spiritual values alone will lead to the salvation of the soul!

This village must be pretty advanced — they have folk dances here for entertainment just as we have in the city!

There must be some mistake. I am not fasting. I am starving!

You said your room should have priority — it is complete, Sir.

No,-it is not true that we've lost interest in this project. In fact the Russians showed great interest for three years, the Japanese for two years, later the British, and now, again, the Russians are showing tremendous interest ...!

Sorry for interrupting you when you are talking, Sir. It is not, "... I told to you last time ...", it is, "... I told you last time..."

No, these people are broad-minded — they don't resent your speaking in English or Hindi or Tamil — they just resent your speaking!

Look, another one! That shows our ancients must have had a roaring trade in cottage industries and curios!

He is quite honest, incorruptible and all that, but, unlike the rest of the staff, he goes on complaining about the salary scale.

I am not hiding here, I am living here!

He's the art critic — he knows so much about art, I've asked him to paint my pictures for me!

Actually this contains nothing except my old shaving kit and a couple of ties...

Stupid charges! Absolutely false! It is very unfair — my son never used influence or pulled wires to get the licence! I gave it to him.

I know, Sir, I should have brought him on the stretcher — but there's such a shortage of hands!

Anything can happen these days! Look at this legal loophole for instance, I bought this flat because I was assured it had a clear sea view!

My dear chap, some V.I.P. is bound to visit this place! The flood has created havoc here, you see!

The only living index of the poorest class I could get, Sir, is that they are living!

True, gentlemen, the model has become popular — what about the soap?

My mission was an utter failure! I've to go abroad again!

There seem to be quite a lot of anti-social elements here — find out who those mischief-mongers are who want to raise the question of food, inflation, water supply etc....!

Yes, it's a mistake! It should be 'Charity Show' but I suggest we leave it as it is till you finish your performance!

I have prepared this simple chart to show population increase, food scarcity, price spiral, sugar scarcity, growth of corruption, unemployment — all in one.

He's my typist — a funny system in this office is the higher officers are not entitled to any D.A.

Why did you ask them to come with specific demands? Those workers only came in to fix the fan which is out of order!

That's the proprietor!

A unique aspect here is that the workers have completely given up the agitational approach to get their demands!

Ah, there he is again! How time flies! It's time for the general election already!

Hold it! Don't, don't! I received news that he is no longer the chief minister. The opposition member has just toppled him!

Further up. Up, a little to the right and up — that's it! — And now let us set about achieving it!

We are all here, Sir — fertilizer supplier, pest controller, seed adviser and soil tester — but I wonder who that man is standing over there!

Those are false allegations that the opposition makes! — Please, believe me, for the hundredth time I repeat, I honestly have no jewels, land, property —!

— *wiped out corruption, improved the lot of the common man, brought prosperity and plenty, when he governed as the chief minister between 17th March 1967 AD and 24th March 1967 AD.*

— and the storage problem is so acute that we are left with no alternative but to give it to the people to eat —

'I must be close to the common people, live like them, eat what they eat —' he said, and was away just for a day, Doctor—!

Yes, I could have taken you by another route — but all other routes are absolutely deserted.

I resigned from the Congress because it had departed from the Gandhian ideals like simple living, self-sacrifice, humility —

I have called you all here to tell you that you have got to manage by yourselves and that there will be no more additions to my staff —!

But they have started washing, bathing, cooking, drinking —!

I know it is a bit elementary for this class — but they threaten to riot if I make it any tougher!

— *these figures I have given are wrong. I have given them because we do not have the right figures —*

Whatever it is, he at least takes decisions!

— *And in this I have tried to convey all my inner tension, struggle and torment!*

Sorry to make you wait, Sir. There is some confusion in the protocol about the way to receive you.

I knew someone was bound to come up with that idea. He is saying, 'English is essential, I admit — but ways and means should be found to teach it in regional languages...'!

I only read out that the police have seized the books and records of a big business firm.

Yes, I said there was no unrest, there was no crisis, there was no unemployment and so on. But surely nobody will take all that seriously — everyone knows it was only a speech.

Oh, we are just two of us here — but being in the fixed income group I can maintain only half the family on the salary I get.

He walked out with us as a protest against them! Now he walks in as a protest against us.

Thanks a lot — now I will tell you why I resigned from that party and why I want to rejoin the Congress!

What I like is the people's unity in this matter!

Yes, Sir, I just finished a thorough study of the grave food situation in Kerala — it shows the food situation in Kerala is grave!

I told you, the calibre of the new recruits is rather low: that young chap wants to know where the junior management pool is!

...*whatever might be your genuine demand we will not allow arson, looting, destroying public property beyond a reasonable limit...!*

I cannot give anything for relief. Whatever I collect goes to maintain this organization!

You don't have to promise them anything, Sir. This is not what has been declared a famine area — it is further up!

Now, remove that and fix this one.

We are so good and did so much for the people — and yet we lost the elections! Why? Because something is seriously wrong with our people!

You mean to say that you placed this note here a month ago? And yet you never bothered to draw my attention to it?

I thought of this because I found it tiring to demonstrate every day for one thing or another!

Don't jeer at me. Jeer at him — he wrote the speech!

I think this region has been neglected for quite a long time: they are singing 'God Save the King'!

One of you is my son. I want him to come home with me.

Of course, socialism is applicable to us also. But we promised it to the people and we must give it to them first!

...and the ruler goes on to assure his subjects that he will eradicate poverty, unemployment...

You have to apply for relief on the prescribed form in triplicate and two witnesses, one a J.P., must endorse it and all applications should be sent by registered post...

He says, since no one in the corporation has the information, he has come to help the passengers!

Oh yes, this village has improved a lot, sir — it's almost like a big city now — no water, no electricity here either!

On the sixth you are abolishing unemployment, Sir. On Tuesday next we are getting rid of poverty, on the fifteenth, bringing down the prices, on...

'Animal husbandry' is the next item — it is bound to be thrilling after this!

You find the country colourful, exciting, rich and full of nice people, madam? Well, I wouldn't know — I am only a tourists' guide.

No, Sir, this famine has not affected us. We have always starved here, you see.

That young professor wants a swivel-chair in his room — otherwise he threatens to emigrate to Canada!

It's terrible, I know. Once I belonged to the fixed income group myself.

Of course we have progressed a great deal, first they were coming by bullock-cart, then by jeep and now this!

I have no problem in running the institution smoothly — luckily not a single student joined this university.

I think the vulgar display of wealth at our daughter's wedding was much better.

...*this exquisitely carved temple belongs to the sixth century and has great antique value. Right now the police are looking for it...*

As you ordered, I have removed all your personal papers from here, Sir.

He is one of the uneducated unemployed and wants a job. Let him deal with those files and dispose of them.

That's why I said he must be new to the city! He has cut it, thinking it works.

Good God! Is he the new one? Before he defected I used to chase him out whenever he came here to hold protest demonstrations!

They should have a separate finance minister for the other economy!

President of which great country, Your Excellency?

See what you have typed! 'That's another ball from Arnold... Gavaskar reaches out and drives it all the way for four'! I asked you to switch that off while I dictated!

He was a great Congress leader! Look, I mean the one below the statue.

I got it done, Sir. The idea, I understand, is to give a cheerful new look to the whole place!

Stay a moment, please! I renewed the pledge, deplored the persistent delays but forgot to show concern about the rising prices...!

And mine is 30% cotton and 70% myself!

I think we would do well to cut out this idea of welcoming the visitors in our cultural costumes!

Quick! I want to end the speech on a note of warning — can you suggest something?

Stop him from shooting it. We have totally banned showing violence on the screen.

I am the most experienced chap here. I have been removing poverty and unemployment for nearly thirty years now!

I did it to set an example in simplicity to them. It's nearly a year now and they have not caught the point yet!

Considering the size of the donation I have given to get my son a seat here, I am not going to let my boy sit in any ordinary seat!

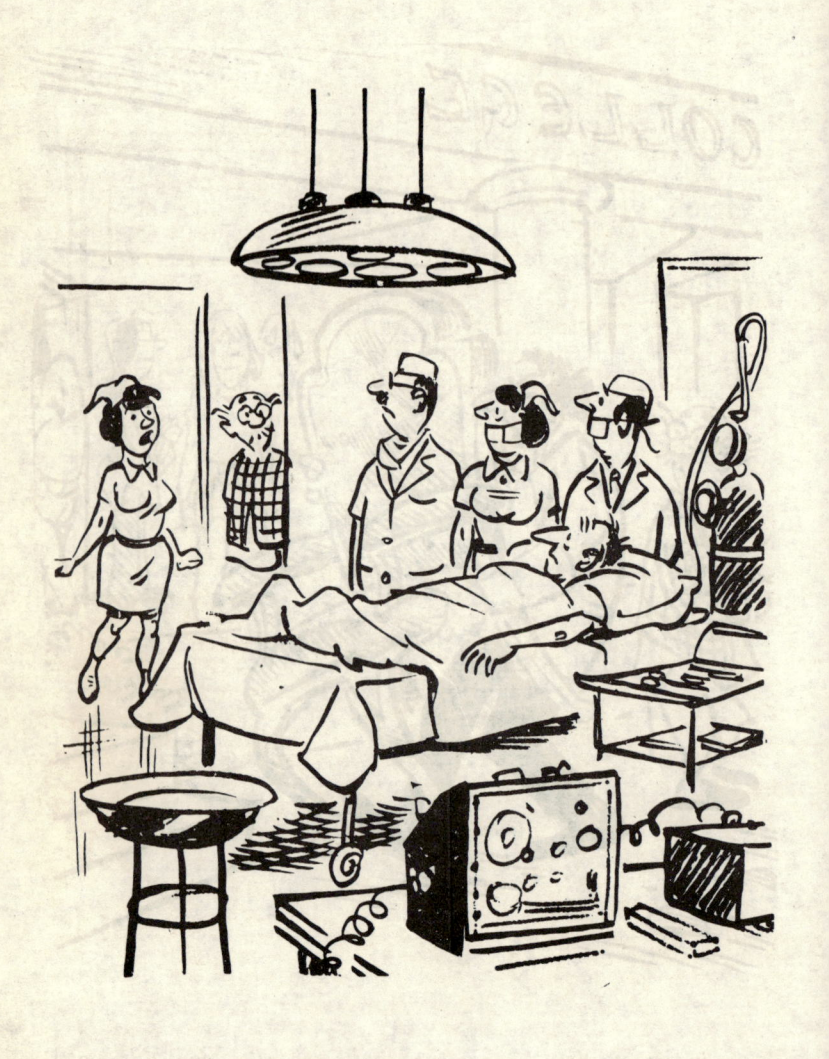

He just sent word he won't be coming; he had to rush to yet another international conference of surgeons!

It is incorrect. You have taken the number of ministers into calculation. That is why the average shows an increase in the number of people who are better fed, sheltered and clothed.

Of course, it's killing, but I am supposed to be a tourist attraction!

That was a spirited, fighting speech, Sir! May we know the subject, please?

Yes, of course it works. It worked on May 4th, June 21st, and again on the second of this month.

I analyzed the loaf, Sir. It is not adulterated. It's pure sawdust!

Yes, it's the one you released a long time ago. But not a single copy was sold. That's why I have requested you to release it again!

Whose pulse is this, please!

That's about the whole village, is it? Couldn't you find some place where I could have delivered this speech on the dangers of the population explosion?

He says he has come in response to a very old invitation extended to him when he was the supreme head of his country before the military coup.

He has a point there. Instead of renovating it, why not put up five-star hotel close by and make this ruin a tourist attraction

Sorry, miss! Sex and violence are banned and so a slight change had to be made. We have dropped you and substituted him in your place.

No, I don't want these biscuits. I want those gold biscuits that daddy kept under the bottom of that box.

He has become a nuisance. Ever since he has stopped being corrupt, he has started borrowing all the time.

Nobody knows what these are! The agreement with the foreign country is that we export what it wants; and in return it gives us what we don't have. We certainly don't have these!

He must have complete rest: strict doctor's orders, no visitors — except party secretaries, ministers, MPs, VIPs, CMs, etc.

Five stars! Remove a couple of them. I don't like staying in five-star hotels!

Yes, the stars are in your favour. You can submit your resignation now without any fear that it would be accepted!

Of course, I am travelling alone. My wife is accompanying me because I am not well and my son is coming to help her and his wife couldn't be left alone.

Films should not show crime, poverty, violence, corruption, sex, cruelty, misery, but must reflect reality and truth.

According to our statistics, Sir, 50% of the population lives below the poverty line in utter misery and 50% above the poverty line in utter misery.

Here is Rs 98 of the Rs 5,000 loan — the rest was distributed among those officials who helped me to get it!

You will be pleased to know, sir, that we have renamed them all after the heroes and heroines of our nation!

The dacoits around here are very advanced, Sir. Besides country-made guns they make country-made tanks also!

Come on, now why take all this trouble? Just flattery would do, I say!

As you ordered they have patched up their quarrels — but effective only from next week and not immediately, they say!

Want some water to drink, sir? You have to wait till you fulfill the promise you made during the last elections!

Careful, it's very precious! What you have there is about one square foot of land which is about Rs 1,000 around here!

See, he has extended an invitation to visit his country. Find out where it is and fix a date!

This is dead. That receives wrong calls. In this you can hear cross-talk. From that one you can dial wrong numbers.

Yes, he specially ordered it. He is so used to that particular type, he finds it difficult to sit in any other chair!

No care for public feelings these days! In our time we used to call the same thing study tour or export promotion mission...

The chap had counted up to 178245 when we found the snag, Sir. He was counting up instead of counting down!

Sunil, Raju, Usha, Nalini — now hold on tight! — Another huge pot-hole ahead!

He loves the city too much. I told you he wouldn't have the nerve to go through with it!

I have done nothing to improve the lot of the people in my constituency, because I don't want the opposition to say I did it to catch votes!

Did you meet any great scholars, poets, thinkers, scientists when you visited Siberia, Sir?

I know I get rotten advice all the time, but I cannot sack my advisers! They are my aunt, son-in-law, cousin, nephew...!

I can't understand these people. Not a soul here knows how to read or write and yet they want a school.

Looks like we have to use something else on the next generation. People are already getting immune to these.

It's no use signing this pact with his excellency, Sir. The BBC says the rebels have overthrown his regime this morning.

I stoned and damaged public property as a protest against unemployment. I might land a job by the time I grow up, you see, if I start agitating right from now.

He has definitely lost his hold over the Worker's Union.

My son, Sir? Oh, he is doing very well, thank you. He is a beggar in Bombay!

My, my, what has happened? Your career line was clear and straight only yesterday! Today it looks thin and wobbly?

Yes, Sir, I let him go. He threatened to inform the higher authorities if I didn't!

Why Sir, it's your portrait. Got it done specially for this Convention!

... And he has the welfare and prosperity of our nation at heart. He is truly a patriot. He is no ordinary Indian. He is a non-resident Indian!

This is clearly to hit the cartoonists!

Father, I've again failed! Could I now drop-out and enter politics, please?

He just walks in without demonstrations, slogans, threats, without even a memorandum and asks for prices to be brought down! — What cheek!

I had it painted. I was tired of saying 'I have no information' over and over again.

Oh, the suffering I went through during our regime! I became corrupt, misused the funds, amassed wealth... I am glad it's all over now!

I can't call ours a developing country. It is really a poor one. We don't even have pollution, unemployment, inflation, over-population...

Don't be unreasonable, I say. The rest of the text books are under print. You will get them when they are ready!

But, Sir, you said I should take bold decisions myself and not run up to you for advice all the time!

We wanted to present you with a purse, really, but our collections were just enough to buy only the purse!

I have been watching, Sir, if you keep passing the files between you two what's to happen to my job?

I see that you are earning beyond your means!

Our pitch occupied again! At this rate the future of cricket in this country is doomed!

He has not changed a bit. When we saw this movie 30 years ago he fell asleep exactly the same way in the theatre!

I don't know if the king disclosed his wealth, I don't know if his land came under the ceiling, I don't know of the price asked for dowry — stop asking questions and listen!

It's aerated water someone hurled at him! I am not surprised; anyone would be thirsty making that long boring speech!

You say you have been fighting for justice, fair-play and human rights for the past 20 years and yet you couldn't set fire to a simple city transport bus!

Why are you clearing it. Any VIP visiting the city?

This is the only road available from your residence to your office, Sir. All the others are taken up by demonstrators!

No, he is not in. But I can tell you unless you withdraw the allegations there is no use talking about any compromise.

When I was in the opposition I believed that the government was ruining the nation. Now that I am with the ruling party I can see that it is the opposition which is doing it!

All this was a park once. Now, I think, even this seat will go making room for more buildings!

Get this speech typed afresh and insert new jokes for old ones!

I don't know whom to blame now. If we had filled that vacancy we could have held him responsible for this muddle and sacked him!

It's like in our movies — sex and violence!

Actually this function has no connection with anything in particular. The chief guest has no engagement today so we fixed this!

It is a crucial meeting strictly between them without even interpreters. But they don't know each others' language!

Excuse me, Sir, could we have the garland back for the next VIP?
Your orders are to economize spending on these things!

Inflation has gone up, no doubt, but nothing to panic. We kept it under control when it was 5%. We will keep it under control at 13% level now.

Luckily nobody noticed it, Sir! The speech you made on Republic Day was the same one you delivered last year!

A hawker! — Must have got a stay order from the Supreme Court.

I swear I was not airing anti-party views! All that I said was that the steep price hikes of essential goods might add to the burden of the common man!

The financial crisis in this state must be truly grim, Sir. The chief minister has written a post-card desperately asking for help!

Eight killed on Tuesday, Ten on Friday! Sunday twenty. That shows they are progressively getting more and more frustrated and it won't be long before they give up and surrender!

If you cut down on these wasteful expenditures he is bound to notice it and you will get into trouble. Cut down on essentials and he won't know!

He is in a fix! As a successful lawyer he has excellent arguments in support of the strike. But he has an equally brilliant one against it!

Yes, Sir, it was a good crowd — 75,622! Of which 57,794 were our own organizers and 17,820 were security men!

Just ignore it, I say. Probably the fools don't know your popularity rating is more than 87%!

What do you mean you can't think of a place to keep it? Surely you are not keeping that thing here till the next elections?

No, my dear boy, 'killed, killed, killed ...' not now. The news is at nine thirty!

*Sorry to have made you come running, Sir! I meant **A N**ative of **R**ural **I**ndia when I phoned to say an NRI was here to see you.*

Shall I switch it off or do you want to sleep!

It is a simulator for passenger training. They are asked to board, sit inside for a couple of hours and then asked to get off. It is to get them used to our service!

Kidnap, murder, assault, blackmail ... can't you people talk anything except politics?

He has started practising some simple tunes. He thinks if his perks are cut he won't be able to entertain his clients any other way!

I have worked out some interesting figures — 12.8%, 14.7%, 1.5% only, 22.3%! Incorporate these in my speech.

Gone up from rupees four to twelve, has it? Never mind. Buy it. The finance minister has assured us this hike won't affect us, anyway!

My new adviser is extremely good, no doubt. But I don't like everyone coming to visit me going to him straight!

I am air-dashing to Delhi! If anyone wants me I will be in the airport lounge for the coming six ... ten ... or even sixteen hours or so.

Why did I call him, 'Young man'? Because he belongs to the Youth Congress!

Other husbands bring lots of money after horse trading. Politics is not your line, I tell you!

Yes, I saw that. Now think of committing yet another blunder so that people may forget this one.

Put it down! Food, water, school etc. granted! I think it was our mistake arming you chaps for self-defence against anti-social elements!

Amazing change for the better! Before entering politics he used to harass the civic authorities with demonstrations and morchas demanding the removal of this slum!

Unless he is given some good tonic soon he will never be able to go to school!

No, he won't fall into the pit! He is quite used to playing around here ever since he was born five years ago!

... Their performances are appreciated not only abroad but in our country also!

Don't be too ambitious, son. I only have some building property, investments, fixed deposits, jewellery etc. I can't afford to pay the capitation fee for your higher education.

... *This injury is the result of the second lathi-charge during the demonstration held to protest against the first and this when demonstrating against the second, and...*

We will shift the garbage temporarily to the other pavement and bring it back later. They are going to dig up this pavement!

*How was a poor policeman to know that you were not a journalist?
You had a note-book and pen in your hand, didn't you?*

Lies! lies! lies! Nothing but lies! How did you get all those details? I want to know!

He says murder, rape, theft and smuggling charges are pending against him. But we must be careful and get more details before he is admitted to the party!

I never said I would resign! I am a loyal party member. I will never resign. All I said was I would threaten to resign.

I don't think they will object to staying here overnight, Sir. They are quite used to sleeping in the office.

'... to provide work opportunities, food, clothing, shelter...' What I like about the planners is their consistency in helping the poor, plan after plan.

The country is going through pretty bad times, no doubt. But must he show his eagerness to get away from it all this way?

... 21, 22, 23, 24! Why is the security slack today? Usually there are 25 guards!

The nice thing is that nobody here is suffering from any diseases. All are healthy cases of injury in political in-fighting, political rivalry, political clashes ...

I am sorry about the ugly scenes, Sir. Actually 99.5 percent can't read. Only one chap there who can and he is responsible for spoiling our image!

Why should you, Sir? Corruption, cover-up, lying, misrule, bungling etc., can't be sufficient reason for resigning.

And this is a grand old one, Sir. But never implemented. It has always served as an excellent election promise !